YOUNG EXPLORERS
in the Land Where
Jesus Lived

◄ by Marcia Hammond ►

Chariot Books™
David C. Cook Publishing Co.

Chariot Books™ is an imprint of David C. Cook Publishing Co.
David C. Cook Publishing Co., Elgin, Illinois 60120
David C. Cook Publishing Co., Weston, Ontario
Nova Distribution Ltd., Newton Abbot, England

YOUNG EXPLORERS IN THE LAND WHERE JESUS LIVED

Edited by Jeannie Harmon
Book and cover design by Jennifer McGuire
Illustrated by Bill Duca
Maps by Cindy Miller
Illustrations on pg. 24 courtesy of Barry Segal International,
Jerusalem, Israel.
Photos: Dr. D. Kelly Ogden and Dr. Richard Cleave

All Scripture quotations in this publication are from the Holy Bible, New
International Version. *Copyright © 1973, 1978, 1984, International Bible
Society. Used by permission of Zondervan Bible Publishers.*

First Printing, 1992
Printed in Singapore
95 94 93 92 96 5 4 3 2 1

Library of Congress Cataloging-in-Publication Data

Hammond, Marcia.
    Young Explorers in the land where Jesus lived / Marcia Hammond.
        p.   cm.
    Includes index
    Summary: Two boys better understand God's Word and teachings
of Jesus through an introduction to the sights and sounds of present–
day Israel as well as its rich history.
    ISBN 1-55513-065-8
    1. Palestine–Antiquities–Juvenile literature. 2. Israel–Discription
and travel–1981–Juvenile literature. 3. Bible–Geography–Juvenile
literature. [1. Palestine–Antiquities. 2.Israel–Desription and travel. 3.
Bible–Geography.]
    I. Title.
DS111.H29 1992
915.69404'54–dc20   91–18628
                                                                CIP
                                                                AC

TABLE OF CONTENTS

5 ◄ The Journey Begins . . .

9 ◄ Sinai

12 ◄ Negev

14 ◄ Animal Life

18 ◄ Wilderness of Judah

22 ◄ Plant Life

25 ◄ Dead Sea

30 ◄ Jordan Valley

34 ◄ Galilee

38 ◄ Agriculture

42 ◄ Northern Hill Country

46 ◄ Climate

49 ◄ Coastal Region

53 ◄ Central Hill Country and Jerusalem

61 ◄ The Journey Ends

62 ◄ Index

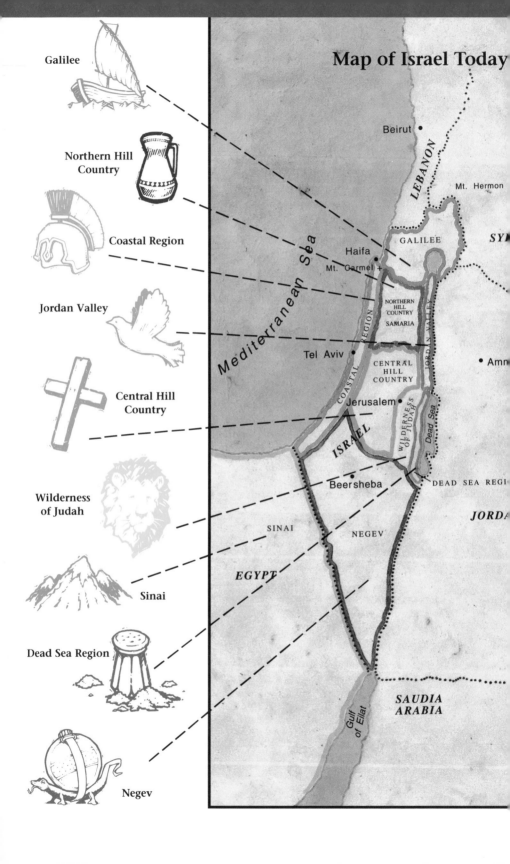

Map of Israel Today

Galilee

Northern Hill Country

Coastal Region

Jordan Valley

Central Hill Country

Wilderness of Judah

Sinai

Dead Sea Region

Negev

Beirut

LEBANON

Mt. Hermon

GALILEE

SY

Haifa

Mt. Carmel +

NORTHERN HILL COUNTRY

SAMARIA

COASTAL REGION

Mediterranean Sea

Tel Aviv

CENTRAL HILL COUNTRY

JORDAN VALLEY

Amm

Jerusalem

WILDERNESS OF JUDAH

Dead Sea

ISRAEL

Beersheba

DEAD SEA REGI

SINAI

NEGEV

JORDA

EGYPT

Gulf of Eilat

SAUDIA ARABIA

Shalom! My name is Daniel. I live in Israel, but I'm not an Israeli. My father teaches geography at the Hebrew University in Jerusalem and we moved here when I was five. I've learned a lot about Bible lands from my dad, but he says there are a lot more exciting facts to discover. (Of course, he's a teacher and he is always saying that about everything!) Sometimes I like to tell other kids about what a great place this is. It's neat to think that Jesus lived here a long time ago.

➤The Journey Begins...

Meet my friend Joseph. His family is visiting from the United States. He wants to learn more about the land that Jesus lived in.

"Joseph, did you know that by studying the land, its crops and climate, we can learn about a country's people? For instance, if we study Bible lands, we can learn a lot about its people, even people who lived long ago like Jesus."

"Ah, come on, Daniel. How can studying trees and fruit and dirt help us know about Jesus?"

"It's simple. The more we know about the things that surrounded Jesus, the better we can understand His teachings. The more we understand His teachings, the better we'll know Jesus Himself.

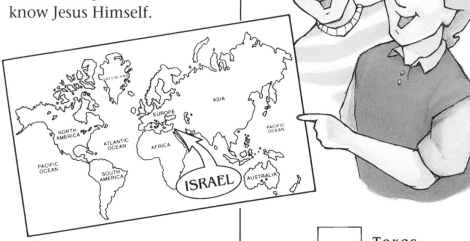

"Let's start by looking at a world map to see where we are. Right here in this little country is where God put His chosen people in ancient times. It has had different names throughout history. One time it was called the Land of the Hebrews. Then it was called the Land of Canaan (K-nun) or Palestine. Today it is called Israel."

"It looks pretty small to me, Daniel."

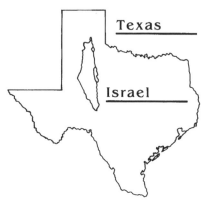

"It is. My dad says that you can fit twenty-five Israels inside the state of Texas. But even though it's small, it has every kind of region from tall mountains to flat, hot deserts.

I brought an ancient map along so we could take a look at how Canaan looked before God's people divided it up."

"Looks like Canaan had some pretty important neighbors, like Egypt and Babylon."

"You're right, Joseph. They were bigger and stronger, and they didn't believe in God. They often gave the Israelites a lot of trouble."

"Daniel, I see that some of the names on this map end with the letters 'e-l.' Is there a reason for this?"

"Yes. All the names of towns in the Bible mean something. You see, Hebrew was one of the main languages used in the land of the Bible and they put words together to make other words. Since God was so important to these people, they often put their word for God, *el* (say it like the letter "L"), in the name. For instance, the Hebrew word *beth* means 'house of.' If you put 'beth' with 'el,' you come up with Bethel or 'house of God.' Bethel was a town north of Jerusalem."

"That's neat. Do you suppose they did that with people's names, too? Your name has *el* in it."

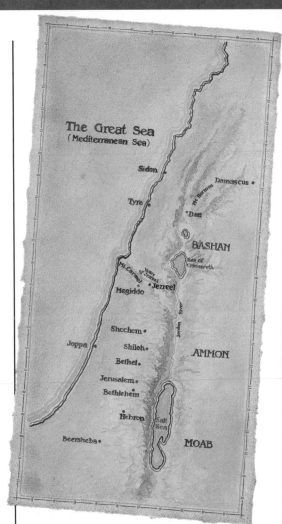

"Right again. *Daniel* means 'God is my judge.' Bible names often had 'el' in them. *Israel*, the name given to Jacob, means 'Prince of God.' *Gabriel* means 'Man of God.' *Michael* means 'One who is like God.' And . . ."

"Ok, ok. I get the picture. There's Bethlehem. I know that city. That's the place where Jesus was born. But it doesn't have an *el* in it. You'd think *that* city would have God in the name."

"Well, Bethlehem was named long before Jesus was born there. My dad says that the word *lehem* means 'bread.' . . ."

"So if you put *beth* which means 'house of' with *lehem* which means 'bread,' you have 'house of bread,' right?"

"You are really catching on, Joseph. Dad says that there were grain fields to the east of the city and bread was made from the grain. In fact, everyone in Canaan ate bread. It was baked fresh daily in clay-brick ovens near their houses. The people would have starved without bread."

Loaves of Bread

➤ Jesus talked about bread when He taught the people. He said, "I am the bread of life" (John 6:35), and "Man does not live on bread alone, but on every word that comes from the mouth of God" (Matthew 4:4). He wanted them to know that there was another kind of bread even more important than the kind they ate. Jesus and His teachings were the other kind of bread. By following His teachings the people would be happy. Jesus, the Bread of Life, came from Bethlehem.

> Sinai

(SIGN-i)

Mt. Hermon

Damascus

SYRIA

LEBANON

GALILEE

NORTHERN
HILL
COUNTRY

SAMARIA

JORDAN VALLEY

REGION

Tel Aviv

CENTRAL
HILL
COUNTRY

Amman

Jerusalem

WILDERNESS
OF JUDAH

Dead Sea

ISRAEL

Beersheba

DEAD SEA REGION

JORDAN

NEGEV

Gulf
of Eilat

*SAUDIA
ARABIA*

"Let's look at a map of Israel today. Even though it is a small country, it can be divided up into regions."

"You mean like the Rockies and the great plains in America?"

"That's right, Joseph. Let's start in the south with the Sinai Desert."

The Sinai Desert

"Daniel, the Sinai looks bigger than the entire country of Israel."

"It is. The Sinai is three times bigger than Israel, but it isn't part of the country of Israel today. It belongs to Egypt."

"Didn't Moses take God's people into the Sinai, Daniel?"

"My dad says that the children of Israel wandered in the Sinai wilderness for forty years!"

"Forty years!"

"You got it, Joseph. Moses led them out of Egypt where they had been slaves to Pharaoh, but God couldn't take them into the promised land because they were so disobedient. They had to wait and learn to obey. They lived in that desert and learned to have faith that God would feed them and help them find water to drink."

"It must have been miserable living in that heat for forty years."

"Not only is it hot, but there isn't much water. Not many plants, trees, or crops grow in the Sinai. Not many people live there either. People settle wherever they can find fresh water. The Sinai doesn't have enough water."

Because of the lack of water, the vegetation is sparse in the Sinai region.

The mountains of the Southern Sinai Region

"Not only that, Joseph, take a look at these mountains in the southern part of Sinai. One of these mountains was the one that Moses climbed to talk with God and receive the Ten Commandments. Dad says that no one knows for sure which mountain it was, but today visitors climb a mountain named Mt. Sinai—which by the way, is 7,500 feet high—to try to feel what it must have been like when Moses was there."

"Looks pretty awesome to me, Daniel."

"Dad says that if you start walking up the mountain early in the morning before the sun is up, you'll have a cool, quiet hike. The moon lights the trail and you'll reach the top in time to see the sunrise. It's beautiful from up there."

> Sinai is a triangle-shaped land bridge between Africa and Asia. It is three times bigger than the State of Israel, running 230 miles north to south and 150 miles east to west. Sinai sits between two branches of the Red Sea: the Gulf of Suez on the west and the Gulf of Eilat or Aqaba on the east. The Gulf of Suez is over 150 feet deep, but the Gulf of Eilat or Aqaba gets as deep as 6,000 feet! It's a lot of fun to go snorkeling or scuba diving in the Red Sea.

> Negev
(NEH gev)

"**M**oving north and to the east, we come to the Negev. The word *Negev* means "dry land." Not much rain falls there, Joseph. Someone said it is so dry that even the lizards carry canteens."

"I'll have to remember that. Dad and I are going to be taking a trip down there soon."

"You can bring me back a picture of one of those lizards. It would fit right in with my collection of strange sights to see."

The Negev

"Many of the Bible stories about Abraham, Isaac, and Jacob that you've read about happened in the Negev. Dad says they lived in a place known as Beersheba (bear-SHAY-vah). *Beersheba* means 'seven wells.' Why do you think Abraham, Isaac, and Jacob dug wells, Joseph?"

"Maybe the wells were their canteens? . . . their water supply?"

"Right again. In a dry region like the Negev, they had to dig into the ground in order to find the water they needed for drinking and to give to their animals and crops."

From Beersheba in the Negev (pictured above), Abraham began his fifty–mile trek with his beloved son, Isaac, to the land of Moriah to offer him for a sacrifice as God commanded. That trial of Abraham's faith and obedience made Mt. Moriah sacred, and hundreds of years later Solomon built the House of the Lord–the holy Temple –at the same place (Genesis 22:1-19 and II Chronicles 3:1).

> Abraham, Isaac, and Jacob, are referred to as patriarchs in the Bible. The word *patriarch* means father. Abraham was the father of Ishmael, and it is from Ishmael that many of today's Arab peoples descend. Abraham was also the father of Isaac, and Isaac was the father of Jacob. God gave Jacob the name *Israel* after Jacob had an all-night wrestling match with an angel (Genesis 32:22-28). So all descendants of Jacob (Israel) were called Israelites, and they are related to the patriarchs Abraham, Isaac, and Jacob.

➤ Animal Life

"Now, Joseph, when I say the word Israel, what animals do you think of?"

"Sheep! Camels and donkeys!"

"Right. But during Bible times there were also lions, crocodiles, and bears. Today none of these animals live in Israel. People moved in, settled so much of the country, and killed animals that they felt threatened their safety."

There are still many donkeys. They were respected animals in ancient Israel. Kings rode them when they were to be crowned. Jesus rode into Jerusalem on a donkey.

The land of the Bible had many sheep and goats, and still does today.

Camels survive well in a desert climate. Because they can store great quantities of water inside their bodies, camels can go many days without a drink of water.

Today there are over three hundred and fifty different kinds of birds in Israel. Israel is on a major bird migration route from Europe to Africa and back.

There were many fish in the Sea of Galilee. Peter, James, and John were fishermen on the Sea of Galilee. Jesus told them to leave their nets, follow Him, and become fishers of men instead. He wanted them to teach people the Gospel so that many others would be saved. Today the Sea of Galilee still provides a major fishing industry.

The locust is the insect most referred to in the Bible. When the people forgot God, He sent swarms of locusts to plague them. A swarm of locusts could eat four hundred tons of grain a day!

The Wilderness of Judah (JEW-duh)

"It looks like the wilderness is on our schedule next, Joseph. This part of Israel is called the Wilderness of Judah. Dad says that the western part is used for raising sheep and goats, but the eastern part is barren. There is little water and it's rough ground to hike over. Poisonous snakes called vipers, scorpions, and some wild beasts live there."

"Sounds like my kind of place, Daniel."

"It still looks like a wilderness today. It's very much the same as it was in Jesus' day."

< 18 >

> When the Israelites left Egypt they moved through Sinai with banners and symbols representing each tribe. The tribe of Judah used the lion as its symbol (Genesis 49:9).

The wilderness was a frightening place to the people of the Bible. The Old Testament prophets were always warning the people to be obedient to God or He would destroy them and their cities. The prophets warned that wicked cities would become like the wilderness, nothing would grow and no one would want to live there anymore. (Isaiah 64:10; Jeremiah 4:7)

> **Things that happened in the Wilderness of Judah:**

- David herded sheep in the wilderness near Bethlehem for several years.

- David killed a lion and a bear there while he was still a shepherd.

- John the Baptist taught there.

- Jesus fasted and prayed there before He began His teaching.

> After His baptism, Jesus was "led by the Spirit in the desert" (Luke 4:1)*, and while there He was tempted by the devil. Jesus overcame the temptations to use His divine power in wrong ways, and He finished His spiritual preparation to start teaching the Glad Tidings.

* The King James Version uses the word *wilderness* in this Scripture.

➤ Plant Life

The Bible talks about more than one hundred different plants (flora). No other country in the world has so many different kinds of plants in such a small area. It has more than 2,250 kinds of plants. England has 1,700. Egypt has 1,300. And these countries are much larger than Israel. One hundred fifty of Israel's 2,250 plants are found only in Israel and nowhere else in the world.

Thistles

"There is an interesting plant, Joseph. It is a thistle. Thistles are everywhere in the country. Dad said Jesus asked, 'Do people pick grapes from thornbushes, or figs from thistles?' " (Matt. 7:16)

"What does that mean, Daniel?"

"Jesus was saying that just as thorns and thistles cannot grow grapes or figs, neither do evil people produce good deeds."

"Here is an interest-
ing looking thistle called
the galgal plant."

The word *galgal* (gall-gall) means "a rolling thing." It grows fast and strong to begin with and then it turns into a frightening, thorny monster. Its leaves and buds become covered with sharp thorns. In the summer, it begins to dry up, but it still looks pretty mean. Then a strange thing happens. When it looks its very strongest, the plant separates from its roots. With a puff of a summer wind the whole galgal plant blows away.

In Isaiah 17:13, God told His people that their enemies would be like the galgal plant: fierce, strong-looking and mean. But because their enemies were wicked they would be swept away as easily as the galgal plant.

* The NIV version uses *tumbleweed* instead of *galgal*. *Tumbleweed* would be the western counterpart of the *galgal* plant.

< 24 >

➤The Dead Sea

"Joseph, you had better hold your breath. We're going below sea level now."

"But Daniel, I don't see any water. We're not going underwater."

The Dead Sea is called the Salt Sea in the Bible.

"I'm just teasing about holding your breath. But we really are going below sea level. We're at the Dead Sea now. It is the lowest region on the whole earth. Dad says that the Dead Sea is 1300 feet below sea level.

And the deepest part is also 1300 feet deep. "

"Let's see, if you add those two together, Daniel, the bottom would be 2600 feet below sea level."

"Right, and only twenty miles from the Dead Sea is Jerusalem, which is 2600 feet *above* sea level. That's a difference in altitude of nearly one whole mile!"

"That's a pretty fast drop, I'd say."

"The southern part of the Dead Sea is only eight to ten feet deep. Dad says some scholars say that the wicked people in the cities of Sodom and Gomorrah are buried under the shallow end of the Dead Sea."

"Daniel, I remember that

The shallow end of the Dead Sea.

Sodom and Gomorrah were so wicked the Lord had to destroy them. Some messengers from God warned them first and gave Lot's family a chance to get out, but only Lot, his wife and two daughters made it out in time."
(Genesis 19)

"And Lot's wife looked back and turned into a pillar of salt."

The salt in the water causes the plants to have a shell of salt.

➤ The Dead Sea region is one of the driest climates in the world. Its yearly average rainfall is only two inches.

"Joseph, this region used to be well watered and beautiful. But when God destroyed Sodom and Gomorrah, He cursed the land. Now nothing grows. Few people or animals can live here."

"I can see why, Daniel. Everything looks dead."

"It's dead because there's no way for the water to run out. The Jordan and other streams empty into the Dead Sea, but there is no way for the water to leave because the land forms the bottom of a valley."

"Could I swim in the Dead Sea, Daniel?"

"Why not! Lots of tourists come every day to swim here. Well, actually they come to float in the Dead Sea. Some believe

➤ For many centuries six million tons of water have emptied into the Dead Sea every day. Because it's so hot in this region, the Dead Sea loses about the same amount of water daily to evaporation. In other words, six million tons of water evaporate off the Dead Sea each day!

that the minerals and salt in the water can cure skin diseases. Be careful, Joseph. You can't go under in this water. The salt will burn your eyes."

➤ The low altitude makes the Dead Sea region richer in oxygen than any other place on earth–10% more than at sea level. The Dead Sea itself has the highest amount of salt and other minerals of any body of water in the world–over 30%. There is eight times more salt and minerals in the Dead Sea than in ocean water. It has so much solid matter in it that it is heavier than the human body, and that's why people float!

En Gedi

"Joseph, there are two more important places that we should talk about while we are here. They are located on the western shore of the Dead Sea.

"One spot is called En Gedi (n-GEH-dee). As you climb up into the cliffs by the Dead Sea, you can find beautiful springs and waterfalls. This is where David hid from King Saul when Saul was trying to kill him. At one point Saul was in a cave asleep and David had a chance to kill him, but David would not take the life of the Lord's anointed. He still respected the position of a king (I Samuel 24).

"David also hid from Saul at a place called Masada (muh-SAH-duh). Masada means 'stronghold'"(I Samuel 24:22).

➤ The Dead Sea Scrolls

Near the northwestern shore of the Dead Sea is an ancient place called Qumran, where people lived who wrote the Dead Sea Scrolls. One day in 1947, an Arab shepherd boy was looking for some goats that had wandered off, when he discovered some clay jars containing scrolls in a cave. The scrolls were writings on animal skin written about the time of Jesus. From 1947 to 1955, over 850 scrolls were found in eleven caves near Qumran, and nearly half of the scrolls were copies of biblical books. Archaeologists (ark-ee-ALL-uh-gists), the people who dig up things from ancient times, say that these writings are the greatest find of our century! The people who lived at Qumran had broken away from other Jews living in Jerusalem. The Dead Sea Scrolls tell us about some of what they believed and how they survived in the desolate wasteland near the shore of the Dead Sea.

Over 900 Jews on Masada held off the Roman army for three years. The Jews had plenty of water and food in underground cisterns and storehouses. They could have lasted many more years. When the Romans finally broke through, they found that nearly all of the people had killed themselves so that they wouldn't have to become slaves to the Romans. (A.D. 70-73)

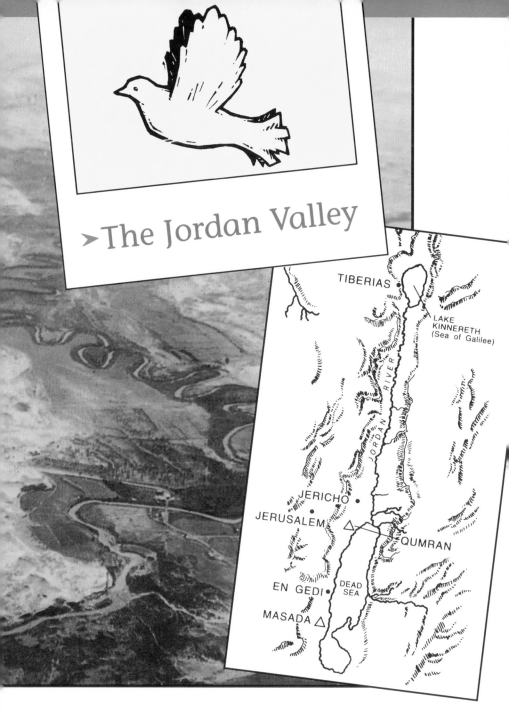

The Jordan Valley

"Joseph, you'll love this next place I'm going to show you. It's the Jordan Valley. Dad says that there is no other spot on this earth quite like it. It connect two lakes, the Sea of Galilee in north Israel and the Dead Sea which is in the south.

"This is the Jordan River. Although there are only seventy miles between the Sea of Galilee and the Dead Sea, the Jordan runs over 200 miles. It moves back and forth like a snake."

Jordan River

"That's a long river, Daniel."

"Actually, the Jordan is not a very long river. Dad says the Nile in Egypt flows over 4,000 miles! The Tigris (TY-grus) and Euphrates (you-FRAY-tees) in this part of the world and the Missouri and Mississippi Rivers in America are all many hundreds of miles long.

"But Joseph, the Jordan is certainly the most famous river in the whole world. It is known and loved and sung about by millions of people who've never seen it. It's sacred because of the special things that happened here."

"Daniel, isn't the Jordan River the river that Jesus was baptized in?"

"That's right, Joseph."

"Can anyone be baptized in the Jordan?"

"Sure. Dad says that Christians come from all over the world to be baptized here."

➤ **Important things that happened at the Jordan River:**

- Joshua parted the waters so that the children of Israel could cross over into the promised land. (Joshua 3:14-17).

- Elijah and Elisha each made the waters of the Jordan part so they could cross on dry ground. (II Kings 2:8,14).

- John the Baptist baptized Jesus in this river. (Matthew 3:13-17).

➤ "As soon as Jesus was baptized, he went up out of the water. At that moment heaven was opened, and he saw the Spirit of God descending like a dove and lighting on him. A voice from heaven said, "This is my Son, whom I love: with him I am well pleased." (Matthew 3:16,17)

> Galilee
(GAL-uh-lee)

Galilee

"Joseph, if I say the word *Galilee* what do you think of?"

"Oh, a big lake, fishermen, and Jesus walking on the water."

"Dad says that nearly three million people lived in the region called *Galilee* at the time of Jesus. There were at least twelve towns around the Sea of Galilee. Chorazin (KOR-uh-zin), Bethsaida (beth-SAY-duh) and Capernaum (kuh-PURR-nee-um), were a few of those cities around the lake where Jesus performed many miracles.

"Here is a picture of what Chorazin looks like today. When Jesus left Bethsaida and Chorazin for the last time, He spoke the same judgment over them as He did for Capernaum, so all three cities are just ruins now."

"That's a lot of ruined cities, Daniel."

"I know. In fact, there is only one town on the shores of the Sea of Galilee today. It is Tiberias, named after the Roman emperor."

The Sea of Galilee is about twelve miles long and seven miles wide. It is the lowest fresh-water lake in the world. Jesus did most of His teaching and most of His miracles in this area.

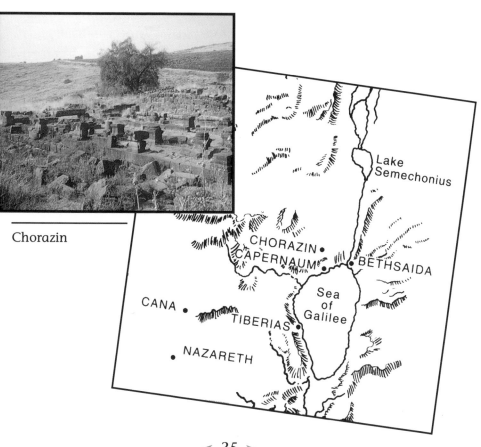

Chorazin

Mango Blossoms near Capernaum

Jesus lived in Capernaum and did many miracles there. Yet most of the people did not believe Him. When He finally left the city, He said, "And you, Capernaum, will you be lifted up to the skies? No, you will go down to the depths. If the miracles that were performed in you had been performed in Sodom, it would have remained to this day. But I tell you that it will be more bearable for Sodom on the day of judgment than for you." (Matthew 11:23, 24)

"Tell me, Joseph, where do you think most of Jesus' apostles came from?"

"I would think from Jerusalem, the biggest city. Right?"

"Actually, Joseph, only Judas Iscariot came from that area. The other eleven of His twelve apostles came from the Galilee region."

Nazareth (NAZ-uh-ruth) is in the Galilee region. Mary probably walked or rode a donkey over the ninety miles from Nazareth to Bethlehem where she gave birth to the Savior. In those days the trip took at least four or five days. It was a hard journey, especially for a pregnant woman. Jesus grew up in the city of Nazareth.

Nazareth

> ➤ Cana (KAY-nuh) was another town in the area. Jesus made water into wine at a wedding party in Cana (John 2:1-11). He also healed the son of a nobleman there (John 4:46-54). Today, the archaeological site where Cana once stood consists of only a few broken down walls.

Agriculture

> **In the Bible it is written,**

"For the Lord your God is bringing you into good land–a land of streams and pools of water, with springs flowing in the valleys and hills; a land with wheat and barley, vines and fig trees, pomegranates, olive oil and honey; a land where bread will not be scarce and you will lack nothing; a land where the rocks are iron and you can dig copper out of the hills. *When you have eaten and you are satisfied, praise the* Lord *your God for the good land he has given you."*

(Deuteronomy 8:7-10)

< 38 >

The people in Bible times grew crops of barley and wheat. They also had many olive trees. Olive trees were easy to grow. They didn't need much water and could survive even when there was no rain.

Wheat

Field workers threshing wheat.

Fruit

Figs, pomegranates, and grapes were also grown. Israel has been a good land for growing fruits and vegetables.

A vineyard in Israel

> Grapes grow on vines and when many vines grow in a big field, we call the field a vineyard (VIN-yard). Since the people knew so much about growing grapes, Jesus used the subject of vineyards to teach them a lesson. He said, "I am the vine; you are the branches. If a man remains in me and I in him, he will bear much fruit; apart from me you can do nothing." (John 15:5)

This example was easy for the people to understand. They worked in grape vineyards every year. Those vines that didn't produce good fruit were useless, not good at all. Vines full of sweet fruit were taken care of and watered.

Jesus was telling them that they were like the vineyard. Those who obeyed would produce good fruit–godly character traits like love, joy, peace, and self-control–and please the Lord. Disobedient people would be cut off from God.

< 40 >

A date palm

The land of the Bible is a land of milk and honey. Honey could have come from bees, but probably it was the heavy syrup of dates.

➤ Northern Hill Country

Samaria was the region where Joshua and the prophets Elijah and Elisha lived.

"The northern hill country was called Samaria, Joseph. It didn't have any natural borders to divide Judea and Samaria, like a river or mountain range. It was easy for the Israelites' enemies to attack it."

"Daniel, isn't that where King Ahab lived?"

"Yes. King Ahab was an Israelite but he married Jezebel, who was not an Israelite. She didn't

believe in the God of Israel and hated His prophets. She killed many of them because they condemned her god named Baal."

"Some lady."

➤ The word *baal* means "master" or "owner", and refers to the many gods worshipped by the Canaanites. Even though each locality had its own baal god, the term *Baal* gradually became the proper name for the Canaanite god who ruled the land, crops, and animals. Idols pictured Baal as a warrior holding a thunderbolt spear.

Elijah put the power of Baal to the test when he challenged the 450 prophets of Baal on Mt. Carmel (I Kings 18:17-40). Only the one true God of Israel could send fire to burn up the sacrifice. The Baal god had no power.

"Daniel, I've heard that the Jews and the Samaritans didn't get along too well. Do you know why?"

"Yeah. The Jews looked down on the Samaritans. My dad says that centuries before Jesus' time, Israelites were taken away from Israel by a powerful enemy named Assyria (uh-SEER-ee-uh). The Assyrians brought in people from other parts of their empire to settle with the Israelites who were left. The mixture of people became known as the Samaritans. They claimed to be full-blooded Israelites, but the Jews would not accept them as such."

> Jesus journeyed through Samaria several times even though other Jews avoided that part of the country. His meeting with a Samaritan woman at Jacob's well was a clear signal that His message was also for non-Jews. It was to this woman of Samaria that He first openly declared that He was the promised Messiah, the Son of God (John 4:25,26).

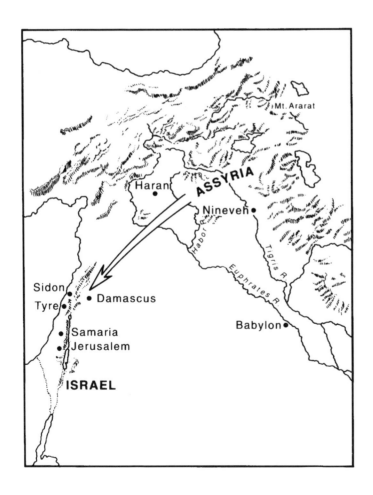

➤ Climate

"**D**aniel, does it ever snow in Israel?"

"Yes, in some places. Israel has only two seasons: a hot, dry season and a cool, wet season. Dad says the cool rainy season lasts only about three months, from January to March, before the hot season comes. Because there is so little rain for the next nine months, the land needs all the rain it can get during the wet season. If you want snow, Joseph, you'll have to travel to Mt. Hermon way up on the northeastern border of Israel."

During the hot months, Israel gets a lot of dew. Dew is water that's in the air. At night this water settles on the thirsty plants. You can see it on the plants.

Some years the land of Israel receives lots of rain and other years it receives very little. It sits at the edge of Europe's storm systems and some years those storms hardly reach Israel at all.

Heavy dew on plants

The people had to learn to trust God to send them the rain they needed. God told them that if they were obedient they would always have enough rain. But many times they forgot God and then it would not rain. The people wouldn't have enough water to grow food or to drink. Lack of food would cause a famine and people and animals would die of starvation.

- Abraham took his whole family to Egypt because there was a famine in the land (Genesis 12:10).

- Elijah asked God to shut the heavens for three-and-a-half years! It didn't rain and a famine resulted (I Kings 17:1).

< 47 >

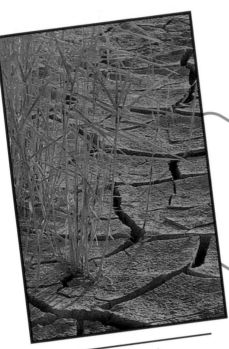

> When the people were
starving and dying, they
remembered God again and
began to repent and be
obedient.

The parched land

> Jerusalem and London
receive about the same
amount of rain each
year. But in London it
rains all year long. In
Jerusalem most of the
rain falls in three months.
Then the hot season
comes and for more
than half a year Israel
gets no rain at all.

< 48 >

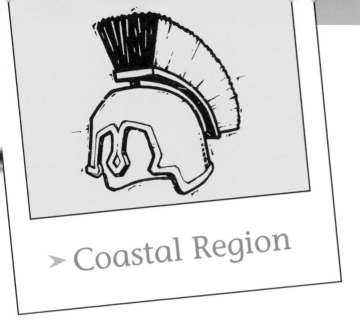

➤ Coastal Region

"It's time to go to the next region, the Mediterranean coast of Israel. It's a very straight coast."

"Great! Maybe we can build some sand castles. Do you think the Israelites went surfing and played in the sand along the beach?"

"I doubt it, Joseph. I think the Israelites were too busy fighting the Philistines.

The western coast of Israel on the
Mediterranean Sea

"It seems that everyone fought with the Israelites."

"Yeah. They had their share of enemies. You see, most of the Philistines lived in the southern part of the coast called the Philistine Plain. They wanted more land so they fought the Israelites to get it."

> The Philistines had a giant hero named Goliath who was over nine and a half feet tall and carried 125 pounds of armor. Goliath challenged any Israelite to come out and fight him, but no one even dared to get close. Then one day a young man named David left tending his sheep near Bethlehem to bring food to his brothers. They were soldiers in the Israelite army. David heard the bragging of the big Philistine bully and decided to take on the giant. He tried on King Saul's armor, but never having fought as a soldier before, David didn't feel comfortable. He decided to go out to meet the giant with only his sling and with his trust in God. Previously the Lord had delivered David from a lion and a bear, so he knew the Lord would deliver him from this Philistine, too.
>
> (I Samuel 17:1-51)

"Joseph, come over here and you can see the same stream where David chose the five smooth stones for his sling."

"Wow! I'm going to take a few of these stones to show my friends. Do you think it would be all right, Daniel?"

"Sure! The land of Israel is so full of stones and rocks that I don't think anyone will miss a few. Did you know that Jesus used rocks as objects to help the people understand His teachings?"

A stream in the countryside

> Jesus said, "Therefore everyone who hears these words of mine and puts them into practice is like a wise man who built his house on the rock. The rain came down, the streams rose, and the winds blew and beat against that house; yet it did not fall, because it had its foundation on the rock." (Matthew 7:24, 25)

> Caesarea (see-zer-REE-uh) was an important port on the Central Coast. It was the Roman capital of Palestine for over 500 years. Philip, Peter, and Paul taught at some time in Caesarea.

Remains of the city of Caesarea. Today it is an historical site.

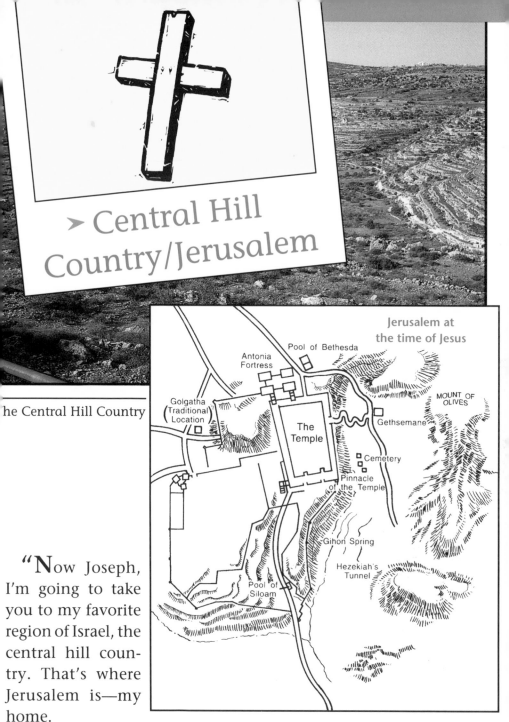

➤ Central Hill Country/Jerusalem

The Central Hill Country

Jerusalem at the time of Jesus

Pool of Bethesda

Antonia Fortress

Golgatha (Traditional Location)

The Temple

Gethsemane

MOUNT OF OLIVES

Cemetery

Pinnacle of the Temple

Gihon Spring

Hezekiah's Tunnel

Pool of Siloam

"Now Joseph, I'm going to take you to my favorite region of Israel, the central hill country. That's where Jerusalem is—my home.

"Dad says that *Jerusalem* means 'City of Peace.' It hasn't been a peaceful place, though. At least fifty battles have been fought there, sometimes the whole city was destroyed. People are still fighting in Jerusalem today."

Major Battles Fought at Jerusalem

➤ David conquered Jerusalem from the Jebusites _____ 1000 B.C.

➤ Pharaoh Shishak raided the city and the temple _____ 940 B.C.

➤ Threatened attack by the Assyrian Sennacherib _____ 701 B.C.

➤ Babylon destroyed Jerusalem and the first temple _____ 586 B.C.

➤ Alexander the Great captured the city _____ 332 B.C.

➤ Maccabees regained the city and temple from Antiochus IV _____ 165 B.C.

➤ Rome destroyed Jerusalem and the second temple _____ A.D. 70

➤ Rome regained control after the Bar Kochba Revolt _____ A.D. 135

➤ Invasion, conquest by Muslims from Damascus (Omayyads) _____ A.D. 640

➤ Other Muslims gained control from Baghdad (Abbasids) _____ A.D. 750

➤ Yet other Muslims (Fatimids) from Cairo _____ A.D. 969

➤ Capture of Jerusalem by Crusaders from Europe _____ A.D. 1099

➤ Saladin overcame Crusaders, ruled from Cairo _____ A.D. 1187

➤ Ottoman Sultan Suleiman gained control for Turks _____ A.D. 1517

➤ British General Allenby established British rule _____ A.D. 1917

➤ Israelis fought for a Jewish homeland _____ A.D. 1947

"Old City" Arab

"With all that fighting, it's amazing that anything is still standing. Why do they fight over Jerusalem, Daniel?"

"Well, it's not just Jerusalem. Today they quarrel about the whole country of Israel. Basically, there are two groups who want to own the land, the Arabs nd the Jews. The Jews say that Israel is the land of their fathers. They claim Abraham as their father. The Jews are descendants of Abraham's son, Isaac. The Arabs also claim Abraham as their father. They are descendents of Abraham's son, Ishmael. The Arabs and the Jews are cousins and they speak similar languages (Genesis 17:19-21)."

"So who is right, Daniel? Who should get the land?"

"Many people believe they are both right, Joseph. But I think the important thing is that God is always for peace. He wants people to work out their differences without fighting and killing each other."

> The town of Jericho, which is only seventeen miles away from Jerusalem, is over 800 feet *below* sea level. That's a drop of 3,400 feet in seventeen miles. In Luke 10:30, Jesus tells the parable of the Good Samaritan. He begins by saying, "A man was going *down* from Jerusalem to Jericho, when he fell into the hands of robbers."

"Hey, Daniel, look at the people over there? They are going into a tunnel. Can we go in, too?"

Jerusalem

"You have to travel up to get to Jerusalem. Remember, it is 2,600 feet *above* sea level."

Gihon Spring

"That's Hezekiah's (heh-zuh-KAI-uhz) water tunnel, Joseph. Dad says that the ancient city of Jerusalem had only one natural source of water. That was the Gihon (gee-HONE) Spring. King Hezekiah built a tunnel from the spring down into the city. Then, when enemies surrounded the city, the people still had water because it flowed into the city through the tunnel."

"Smart move! That was good planning on King Hezekiah's part."

"Right. Today it is called Hezekiah's Tunnel. It's no longer used to supply water but people like to roll up their pants and walk through it. They wear tennis shoes because water still runs across the floor of the tunnel."

"Isn't it kind of dark in there?"

"Yes. They carry candles or flashlights to light their way."

Ancient Jerusalem also stored water in cisterns (SIS-terns) which were under the ground. Some of these cisterns were as big as a room. They could hold thousands of gallons of water.

Hezekiah's Tunnel

Water was also stored in pools. Jesus told a blind man to go and wash in the Pool of Siloam (si-LOH-um) and he would be healed (John 9).

A crippled man had lain by the Pool of Bethesda (beth-THEZ-duh) for many years hoping to be healed by its water. When Jesus saw him, He told him to take up his bed and walk. The man was healed (John 5).

Ancient Jerusalem always had water. Its enemies were never able to cut off the city's water supply.

Pool of Siloam

Mount of Olives

"Joseph, have you heard of the Mount of Olives?"

"Isn't that where the Garden of Gethsemane was, Daniel?"

"Yes. The Mount of Olives is just outside Jerusalem–where the Garden of Gethsemane was. Jesus prayed there just a few hours before He was sent to the cross."

"Daniel, do you think that some of these same trees were here when Jesus prayed in this garden?"

"They could have been, Joseph. If these trees could talk they might have some stories to tell. They are many centuries old."

In ancient Canaan there were some great forests. Over the centuries people cut down almost all the trees for wood. New forests are being planted today. The oldest trees in the country are the olive trees in the Garden of Gethsemane.

"Look over here, Joseph. The Garden of Gethsemane is not all that is on the Mount of Olives.

Olive trees in Gethsemane

It's a graveyard, too."

"WOW! There sure are a lot of graves. Seems like hundreds."

"Dad says you can see more than 70,000 graves on the Mount of Olives. It was easy to make tombs out of the soft, white rock of the mountain."

The cemetery on the Mount of Olives

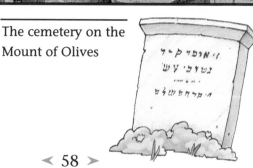

> Jesus said, "Woe to you, teachers of the law and Pharisees, you hypocrites! You are like whitewashed tombs, which look beautiful on the outside but on the inside are full of dead men's bones and everything unclean." (Matthew 23:27, 28)

Jesus knew they would understand Him because beautiful, white sepulchres were common in the land. He was telling them that even though they looked good on the outside, inside they were full of hate and evil.

The Temple Mount

"Over here, Joseph, is the Temple Mount. It was also part of the ancient city of Jerusalem. The Jews built a temple here, but their enemies were able to destroy it because the Jews did not obey God."

"What's this high wall, Daniel? Could I climb it?"

"I don't think so. It's part of the Temple Mount. This whole area is sacred to both Jews and Arabs. It was from a high wall of the Temple Mount that Satan told Jesus to cast himself down and then use His miraculous power to save Himself. Jesus refused." (See Matthew 4:5-7)

The high wall of
the Temple Mount

< 59 >

"The stones along the wall of the Temple Mount are very heavy. Some weigh 150 tons! One stone that was discovered weighs 450 tons!

"That's a lot more than our car weighs. It is only two tons."

> The Temple Mount used to be called Mount Moriah (moh-RYE-uh), the place where Abraham went to offer his son Isaac for a sacrifice. (See Genesis 22.)

> The people asked Jesus for a sign or a miracle that He had power. They were amazed when He said, "Destroy this temple, and I will raise it again in three days." They said, "It has taken forty-six years to build this temple, and you are going to raise it in three days?" (See John 2:19-21.)

They didn't understand that Jesus was talking about His body. The people would kill Him, destroy His body (temple) and He would raise it up after three days.

The Dome of the Rock

"Daniel, doesn't that gold dome belong to the Arabs? What is it doing on the Temple Mount?"

"Joseph, the Muslim Arabs built a beautiful gold-domed building on the Mount because they also believe that Abraham offered a sacrifice here. But they believe he offered Ishmael, his other son, and not Isaac (Genesis 22)."

< 60 >

> The Journey
   Ends...

"Joseph, my dad comes close to crying sometimes when he thinks about all that happened in this one tiny place on earth. The land where God chose to put His people and His dwelling place (the temple), was made "holy" by the prophets and the apostles and by God's own Son living and teaching here. Dad tells me that over the centuries it came to be known as the Holy Land because some of the greatest events in 4,000 years of history happened here.

"For sure, the most important things that have ever happened in our world took place in Jerusalem--the death and resurrection of our Savior. Knowing more about the land He lived in helps us to better understand His life and message which can lead us to life forever with Him."

Index

Abraham 13, 47, 55, 60

Africa 6, 11, 16

Arabs 13, 29, 54, 55, 59, 60

Asia 6, 11

Assyria 44, 45

Baal 43, 44

Babylon 7, 45

Beersheba 4, 13

Bethel 7

Bethlehem 7, 8, 21, 37, 50

Bethsaida 34, 35

Bread 8

Caesarea 52

Cana 35, 37

Canaan 6, 7, 8, 44, 58

Capernaum 34, 35, 36

Central Hill Country 4, 53

Chorazin 34, 35

Cistern 29, 56

Coastal Region 49

Daniel 7

David 21, 28, 50, 51, 54

Dead Sea 4, 25, 26, 27. 28, 29, 30, 31

Dead Sea Scrolls 29

Egypt 4, 7, 10, 19, 22, 32, 47

Elijah 33, 42, 44, 47

Elisha 33, 42

En Gedi 28, 30

England 22

Euphrates 32, 45

Europe 6, 16, 47, 54

Flora 22

Gabriel 7

Galgal plant 24

Galilee 4, 34, 36, 37

Garden of Gethsemane 53, 57, 58

Gihon Spring 53, 55, 56

Goliath 50
Gomorrah 25, 26, 27
Gulf of Eilat (or Aqaba) 11
Gulf of Suez 11
Hezekiah's tunnel 53, 56
Holy Land 61
Isaac 13, 55, 60
Ishmael 13, 55, 60
Israel 5, 6, 7, 9, 10, 11, 13, 14, 16, 18, 22, 30, 39, 40, 43, 44, 45, 46, 47, 49, 51, 53, 54
Israelites 7, 13, 19, 33, 42, 44, 49, 50
Jacob 7, 13, 45
James 16
Jericho 30, 55
Jerusalem 5, 7, 14, 25, 29, 30, 36, 48, 53, 54, 55, 56, 57, 59, 61
Jesus 5, 6, 7, 8, 14, 16, 18, 21, 23, 32, 33, 34, 35, 36, 37, 40, 44, 45, 51, 52, 55,
    57, 58, 59, 60
Jews 29, 44, 45, 54, 55, 59
Jezebel 42
John 16
John the Baptist 21, 33
Jordan River 27, 31, 32, 33
Jordan Valley 4, 30
Joshua 33, 42
Judah 19
Judas Iscariot 36
Judea 42
King Ahab 42
King Hezekiah 56
King Saul 28, 50
Land of the Hebrews 6
Locust 17
London 48
Lot 26
Masada 28, 29, 30,
Mediterranean Sea 4, 7, 9, 49
Michael 7
Mississippi River 32

Missouri River 32

Moses 10, 11

Mount of Olives 53, 57, 58

Mt. Carmel 44

Mt. Hermon 4, 46

Mt. Moriah 13, 60

Mt. Sinai 11

Nazareth 35, 37

Negev 12, 13

Nile 32

Northern Hill Country 4, 42

Palestine 6, 52

Patriarch 13

Paul 52

Peter 16, 52

Philip 52

Philistines 49, 50

Pool of Bethesda 57

Pool of Siloam 57

Qumran 29, 30

Red Sea 11

Salt Sea 25

Samaria 4, 42, 45

Samaritans 44, 45, 55

Sea of Galilee 16, 30, 31, 34, 35

Sinai 4, 9, 10, 11, 19

Sinai Desert 10

Snow 46

Sodom 25, 26, 27, 36

Solomon 13

Temple Mount 53, 59, 60

Ten Commandments 11

Texas 6

Thistles 23

Tigris 32, 45

Vineyard 40

Wilderness 10, 18, 20, 21

Wilderness of Judah 18, 21